WHAT'S THE BIG IDEA?

SHAPES

Pamela J.P. Schroeder
Jean M. Donisch

ROURKE PUBLICATIONS, INC.
VERO BEACH, FL 32964

A book by Market Square Communications Incorporated.
A special thanks to our creative team, Sandy Robinson, Sandra Shekels and
Ann Garber of Market Square Communications Incorporated, for their creative
text and design contributions.

Consultants:

       Jeanette L. Handrich — M.A. in Elementary Education/Language
            Arts, third and fourth grade teacher/gifted and talented
            program, over 20 years teaching experience
       Karen M. Olsen — M.S. in Education, kindergarten teacher,
            over 20 years teaching experience
       Geri Pape — M.S. in Elementary Education, kindergarten teacher,
            over 30 years teaching experience

Library of Congress Cataloging-in-Publication Data
Schroeder, Pamela J. P., 1969-
   Shapes / Pamela J.P. Schroeder, Jean M. Donisch.
     p. cm. — (What's the big idea?)
   Summary: Illustrations and rhyming text introduce such shapes as
circles, rectangles, triangles, ovals, and polygons. Includes related
questions.
   ISBN 0-86625-577-X
   1. Geometry—Juvenile literature. [1. Shape.] I. Donisch, Jean M.,
1960-   . II. Title. III. Series.
QA445.5.S37   1996
516—dc20   95-52196
                                    CIP
                                    AC

TABLE OF CONTENTS

For more
fun with
SHAPES ideas,
look for the
shape at the
bottom of
the page.

ABOUT SHAPES

When you see your shadow
Up there on a wall,
How do you know who's it is —
If it's yours at all?

It's the shape of the thing,
The curves and the sides,
The outline that helps you
See your shape and decide.

Some shapes have names.
There's square and triangle
And circle and oval
And star and rectangle.

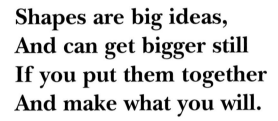

Shapes are big ideas,
And can get bigger still
If you put them together
And make what you will.

This book will help you
See shapes all around —
In your school, in the sky,
In your house, on the ground.

Use the shapes that you find
To build wonderful things.
Shapes can take your ideas
And give them wings!

Bouncing, spinning,
rolling, round —
a circle's never
upside-down!

It has no corners
or sides at all.
Its cousin, the sphere,
is the shape of a ball.

What do people
mean when they say,
"I'm going around
in circles"?

On this shape,
each side is the same.
Four sides and
four corners —
a square is its name.

You can draw squares to
plan on computer screens.
Then use cubes,
like wood blocks,
to build your scenes.

**How many
squares
can you find
on a cube?**

9

TRIANGLE

To make a triangle
is easy as 1, 2, 3 —
three corners
and three sides
are all that you need.

Together triangles
can make a long bridge
or a mighty
Egyptian pyramid.

**What other
objects can
you make by putting
triangles together
in different ways?**

RECTANGLE

SCIENCE IN ART

SCIENCE
IN ART

SCIENCE
PROJECTS

Four corners like a
square, but two sides
are stretched out —
a rectangle's what we're
talking about.

A ruler, eraser,
or folder or book
is exactly how
a rectangle should look.

**Look around the room and find
some rectangle shapes.**

OVAL

If you took a circle and
squashed it a bit,
very soon you'd make
an oval from it.

Long in the middle and
round on the ends,
like a race track
you'd run around
with your friends.

**What other
things are oval?**

DIAMOND

A diamond has four sides
and four corners, it's true —
it's a bit like a square
and a rectangle, too.

But a diamond is special —
it stands on its tip.
Like a kite in the sky,
it has lots of zip!

**What makes
a diamond different
from a square or
rectangle?**

POLYGON

PENTAGON

HEXAGON

OCTAGON

A polygon shape gets its
name from its sides.
They come in all sizes,
some small and some wide.

With your finger, you
can pin polygons down.
Point to each side and
count all around.

**If hepta means seven,
what would a heptagon
look like?**

PARALLELOGRAM

Parallelograms
have two pairs of lines.
Like box sides, they stay
side by side all the time.

Parallel lines
never cross or curve in —
like the boxes you save
for the recycling bin.

**What parallelograms
do you recycle?**

TRAPEZOID

U.S.S. TRAPEZOID

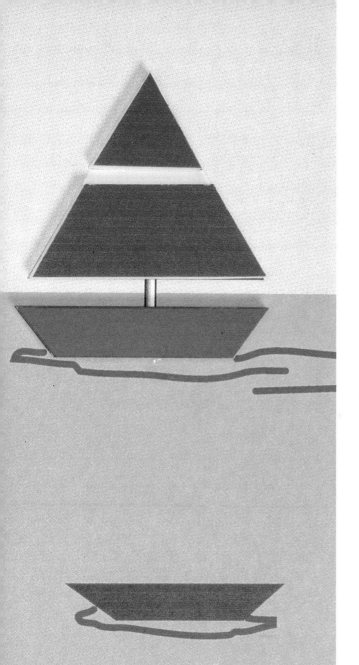

Take a triangle and slice
off the top.
A trapezoid shape
is what you've got.

Two parallel sides,
one long and one short —
like the bottom of a ship
afloat in a port.

Can you draw a picture
using trapezoids?

HEART

Heart shapes are curved,
but they have a point, too.
Most hearts are red —
they cheer you up
when you're blue.

Hearts are happy shapes.
They're shared
between friends.
"I care about you,"
is the message one sends.

Who would you
send hearts to?

STAR

Star shapes have points
that go all around.
Look up at night,
you'll see stars
shining down.

When you're by the ocean,
look down at your feet.
If you're very lucky,
it's a starfish you'll meet.

**Why do you think
famous people
are called
stars?**

WHAT'S THE BIG IDEA? ABOUT SHAPES

Shapes are everywhere —
Outside, inside, on walls, on the floor.
Now that you can find them,
You can do even more.

Your shadow
Is a shape that is flat —
But a shape, given room,
Can be much more than that.

Use a triangle, pyramid,
circle or sphere —
Use octagons, rectangles,
Any shape here —

To build big ideas
That grow in your mind.
There's no limit to shapes —
Don't leave any behind!

GLOSSARY

circle – a round shape, even all the way around

cube – a 3-D shape with six sides; the top, bottom, front, back and sides are all square

diamond – a shape with four equal sides, and corners that can be skinny or fat

heart – a shape that means love and friendship

hexagon – a shape with six sides

octagon – a shape with eight sides

oval – a round shape that is stretched in the middle

parallel – lines that go side by side; they never cross, get closer together, or get farther apart

parallelogram – a shape with four sides — two sets of parallel lines

pentagon – a shape with five sides

polygon – a shape that gets its name from the number of its sides

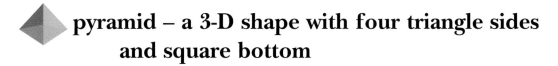

pyramid – a 3-D shape with four triangle sides and square bottom

rectangle – a shape with two pairs of matching sides (four sides altogether) and four corners

shape – the outline, or form, of something

sphere – a 3-D shape that is round like a ball

square – a shape with four equal sides and four perfect corners

star – a shape with points that go all around

trapezoid – a shape with four sides — two parallel sides with one short and one long, and two sides that are the same

triangle – a shape with three sides and three corners

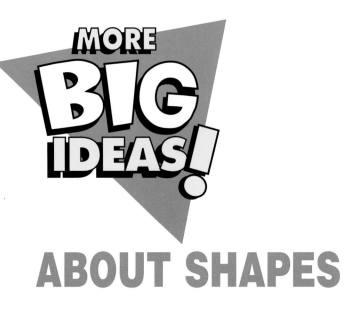

ABOUT SHAPES

Get together with three or four of your friends and try to make the shapes in this book using your bodies.

What would happen if wheels were squares instead of circles?

How many squares can you find in this shape? How many rectangles can you find?

Most buildings are shaped like squares or rectangles. Can you think of buildings made of other shapes?

What shapes do you need to draw an airplane, a skyscraper or a person?

How do *you* remember the difference between a pentagon, hexagon and octagon?